Python for Data Analysis

A Complete Step By Step From Intermediate to Advanced Guide for Python Coding, NumPy, Pandas for Data Analysis. Improve Your Skills Quickly

By
Dany Log

Copyright © 2020 by Dany Log

All rights reserved.

The material contained herein is presented with the intent of furnishing pertinent and relevant information and knowledge on the topic with the sole purpose of providing entertainment. The author should thus not be considered an expert on the topic in this material despite any claims to such expertise, first-hand knowledge, and any other reasonable claim to specific knowledge on the material contained herein. The information presented in this work has been researched to ensure its reasonable accuracy and validity. Nevertheless, it is advisable to consult with a duly licensed professional in the area pertaining to this topic, or any other covered in this book, in order to ensure the quality and validity of the advice and/or techniques contained in this material.

This is a legally binding statement as deemed so by the Committee of Publishers Association and the American Bar Association in the United States. Any reproduction, transmission, copying, or otherwise duplication of the material contained in this work are in violation of current copyright legislation. No physical or digital copies of this work, both total and partial, may not be done without the Publisher's express written consent. All additional rights are reserved by the publisher of this work.

The data, facts, and description of events forthwith shall be considered as accurate unless the work is deemed to be a work of fiction. In any event, the Publisher is exempt of responsibility for any use of the information contained in the present work on the part of the user. The Author and Publisher may not be deemed liable, under any circumstances, for the events resulting from the observance of the advice, tips, techniques and any other contents presented herein.

Given the informational and entertainment nature of the content presented in this work, there is no guarantee as to the quality and validity of the information. As such, the contents of this work are deemed as universal. No use of copyrighted material is used in this work. Any references to other trademarks are done so under fair use and by no means represent an endorsement of such trademarks or their holder.

Table of Contents

Introduction 1

Chapter 1: What is a Data Analysis 5

    What is Data Analytics? 6

    Understanding How Data Analytics Works 9

    The Different Types of Data Analytics 13

Chapter 2: Reasons to Work with a Data Analysis 18

Chapter 3: How Does Python Fit Into This? 29

Chapter 4: Some of the Basic Codes in Python 39

    The Keywords 40

    Python Comments 40

    Python as an OOP Language 42

    How to Write a Class 44

    Python Functions 50

    Python Variables 56

    Lists vs. Dictionaries 58

    Creating a Simple Loop 62

The If Else Statement in Decision Control 63

Can I Create an Inheritance? 67

Chapter 5: What is the NumPy Library 73

Understanding More About NumPy 75

Chapter 6: Taking It Further with Pandas 82

How to Install Pandas 84

The Data Structures in Pandas 85

Chapter 7: The Importance of Cleaning and Organizing the Data 90

Collecting the Data 91

Organizing the Data 93

Dealing with the Outliers 95

Filling in Missing Data 97

How to Deal with Duplicates 99

Chapter 8: Training, Testing, and Repeating 102

Picking Out the Algorithms to Use 103

Training Our Data 107

Testing the Data 108

Repeat the Process 112

Chapter 9: Machine Learning and How It Fits Into Our Data Analysis 116

What is Machine Learning?...............................117

How Does Machine Learning Work with Data Analysis?..122

Supervised Machine Learning 123

Unsupervised Machine Learning.......................125

Reinforcement Machine Learning....................128

Chapter 10: Presenting the Results 134

Conclusion 148

Introduction

Congratulations on purchasing *Python for Data Analysis* and thank you for doing so.

The following chapters will discuss all of the different parts that we need to know when it comes to performing our own data analysis, and ensuring that we are able to really get some good results in the process. There are a lot of different businesses and industries that are able to work with the data analysis and see the amazing results, and it could be just the thing that you need to take your business to the next level. The information and the insights that you are able to find with data analysis will help you to reach your customers better, find the right customers, know what business decisions to make, and so much more.

We will discuss all of these and more inside of this guidebook.

To start this guidebook, we are going to take a more in-depth look at what data analysis is all about. We will talk about this process and what all it entails, along with some of the benefits of working with this process, and why so many businesses are using it for their own needs as well.

When that part is done, it is time to introduce the Python language. It is possible to work with some of the other coding languages out there to help us handle our data analysis, but none of those are going to provide us with the power and the ease of use, and all of the great extensions and libraries specifically for data analysis like Python can. In this guidebook, we will look at how Python can help us complete our data analysis before diving into some of the different things that you need to do, including some of the coding to help you to get started with programming in this language.

Then it is time for us to dive into some of the libraries and extensions that match up to the Python language and were designed specifically to help us with data analysis. There are a lot of great options here, but we are going to talk about the two most important; the NumPy library and the Pandas library. NumPy is important because it contains the arrays that most of the others will rely on, and Pandas is a good library that can help us with all of the different aspects that we need to focus on when it comes to our data analysis. Learning how to work with both of these is going to be imperative to ensure that we will see a successful data analysis.

To finish everything off, we are going to spend our time looking at some of the steps that come with this data analysis. We will be looking at collecting the data and cleaning it. We will be looking at how to pick out our algorithms and get them all set up and trained before testing them. We will even look at some of the steps to help with our visuals so we can see exactly what happened with the analysis and can use that to our benefit later on. There is information about the importance of machine learning in our data analysis so that we are better able to prepare and do well with our work as well.

As we can see, there are a lot of different parts that have to come together to help us complete data analysis and see the results that we want in the process. And this guidebook is going to take the time to look at how we are able to get this done in a quick and efficient manner. When you are ready to learn more about data analysis and how it works, and about the Python coding language, make sure to check out this guidebook to help you get started.

There are plenty of books on this subject on the market, thanks again for choosing this one! Every effort was made to ensure it is full of as much useful information as possible, please enjoy it!

Chapter 1: What is a Data Analysis

Before we are able to dive right in and look at what we are able to do with data analysis, it is time for us to take a closer look at what the data analysis is all about. This is a unique process that a lot of companies are going to work with. It allows them to take the enormous amounts of data they are able to collect on a regular basis today and actually learn some of the insights and predictions that are inside of it.

Doing this on our own is going to be impossible. There is just too much data, and it is changing all of the time. Having an individual, or a team, work through this data is going to be a waste of time and won't provide us with the right results anyway. The data will be old by the time we get to it. Data analysis is a process that is going to be able to help with this.

The data analysis will be able to go through all of the steps that we need in order to understand our data, learn what insights are found in that data, and use it to make some good predictions and more in the process. With this in mind, let's take a closer look at what data analysis is all about and how we are able to utilize this for our needs.

What is Data Analytics?

The first step in this process is taking a look at data analytics and what it is all about. To keep it simple, data analytics is going to be the simple science of taking our raw data and analyzing it in order to make some good conclusions about all of that information. Many of the processes and the different techniques of this kind of analytics have been automated into mechanical processes and algorithms that will be able to do some work over this raw data for human consumption.

The techniques that we are going to use when it comes to data analytics can reveal trends and other metrics that would often get lost in the noise and all of the information that we receive. This information can then be used in a manner to help optimize processes to help increase the overall efficiency of a business or system.

There are a lot of benefits that we are able to see when it comes to working with data analysis. When we decide to bring this out, we will be able to notice how helpful it is, and all of the great parts that come with it as well. it is a simple idea, one that can make a big difference in your business but simple enough to understand, but we have to be prepared to go through and really work with the steps to make it work.

It isn't just about picking out a few algorithms and hoping that it is all going to work. There are a number of steps that we need to go through in order to make the analysis behave, and to ensure that it is going to do what we want, whether we are talking about the work that has to be done before the analysis, the actual analysis, and the work afterward.

For example, when we talk about before the analysis, we have to make sure that we collect the right information and information that is higher in quality, that we clean off the data, and that we get it organized so that it works well with the algorithms we choose. During the analysis, we need to focus on the right algorithm to get the work done, and then do several rounds of training and testing to ensure it works. And after the analysis, finding a good way to show off the results and all that is happening is going to be important as well.

Understanding How Data Analytics Works

Data analytics is actually going to be a term that is really broad, and that will encompass many different and diverse types of data analysis. Any type of information that can be used with these techniques will help us to learn some new insights that will be invaluable. Businesses can use these insights to learn more about their customers, to pick out the best products to release, and even to make smarter business decisions in the future.

For example, it is common for some manufacturing companies to work with data analysis. Many of these companies are going to get into the habit of recording the runtime, downtime, and work queue for lots of different machines. They can then analyze all of the data in order to better plan out the workloads they should do, ensuring that the machine and the whole production line is going to work as closely as possible to its peak capacity.

Data analytics is not just used in order to help point out to those in charge of the bottlenecks in production. For example, we are going to find that gaming companies are going to use this data analytics in order to set some good kinds of reward schedules. This is done in a manner to help keep most of the players of a game active.

Content companies will also work with these data analysis in order to work with some of their customers and help to get the readers or consumers to keep on clicking, watching, moving content around, and more. This gives them another click or another view, and then they will be able to earn more money in the same process.

There are actually a number of steps that we are going to work wit in order to work with data analysis. This is going to include some of the following options:

1. The first step that we want to work with here is to determine the data requirements or how

the data is going to be grouped. Data may be separated by demographics, income, age, or gender. The values of this data may be numerical or be divided by category.

2. The second step that we are going to see when it comes to data analytics is the process of collecting all of the data that we want to work with. This can be done through a lot of sources, and we will be able to utilize as many of these as possible in order to gather the information and get it to work well for our needs. You can use online sources, computers, social media, surveys, and more.

3. Once we have had a chance to collect all of the data we want to work with, we then need to actually organize it all. If the data is not organized, which it won't be, if we gather it from a lot of different sources, then we are not going to be able to push it through our chosen algorithms and get accurate results.

    a. There are many methods that we are able to use in order to organize all of that data.

> We can work with a spreadsheet or other form of software that is able to take on some of the statistical data we want.

4. From this step, we are going to clean up all of the data before we work on the analysis. This means that it is going to be checked and scrubbed to make sure there will be no error or duplication and that it is not actually incomplete. This step is a good one to follow in order to get rid of the errors before it is going to be sent over to the analyst to be looked over and worked on by a chosen algorithm.

These are just a few of the options that we are going to pay attention to when it comes to doing data analysis. There are a lot of different parts that we need to bring this together and ensure that we are able to see how it can work and how those companies who decide to work with it can really use it to get ahead and see a foot above the competition in the process.

Data analytics is going to be an important thing to work with because it allows a business to come in and optimize its performance overall. Implementing this kind of process into your model for business means that it is easier to reduce the costs that are present. The company at hand is able to use it to identify some more efficient methods of coding business and storing a lot of data all at once.

A company is also able to take the ideas of data analytics and use it as a way to make some better decisions for their business, and to help them to analyze some of the customer trends and the satisfaction, which is going to lead to new, and better, products and services.

The Different Types of Data Analytics

We are able to take the idea of data analytics and divide it into four different types to make it easier to see what is going on here. The four types of data analytics that we are able to work with includes

1. Descriptive analytics: This is going to describe what has been able to happen over a given period of time. You may take a look to see whether your sales have gone up over the last month or if your views are going up on a video.
2. Diagnostic analytics: This one is a bit different because it is going to focus some more on the reason why something has happened. This is going to involve some data inputs that are more diverse, and you will need to hypothesize a bit. For example, you may ask whether the latest campaign had any impact on your sales.
3. Predictive analytics: This is going to take a look at what we think is going to happen in the near term. It may look at how sales did the last time the summer was hot, and then it will look at how likely it is going to be really hot during summer again.

4. Prescriptive analytics: This is going to suggest a course of action. If it is likely that we are going to get a warm summer again and we measure it based on an average of five weather models, then you would rearrange your business so that you can keep up with the demand.

Data analytics is going to take some time to underpin some of the other quality control systems that are found in the world of finances. One of these quality control programs that will often work well with data analysis is going to Six Sigma. This is a whole program that helps us to find some of the waste that is found in the business, and then learn how to reduce this to help save money and become more efficient.

The idea with both of these is that if you are not able to go through and measure something properly, whether you are looking at your own weight or the number of defects that are going to show up per million on the production line, then it is going to be impossible for the company to really optimize it.

There are also a lot of different companies that have decided to adopt data analytics in their own business model in order to get some of the best results. One of the first sectors that we can look at that has used data analytics is hospitality and travel. These are going to need a lot of quick turnarounds to see some good results, and this industry is able to go through and collect some data about the customers to figure out where the problems, if there are any problems, lie, and how we are able to fix them early on.

Another place where we are going to be able to see the benefits of data analytics in the world of healthcare. This is going to be able to combine together the use of high volumes of structured and unstructured data, and then will work the data analytics and all of the techniques that come with it to help make some smart decisions.

In a similar manner, the retail industry, which may be an industry that we don't think that much about when it comes to working in data analytics, is going to work here as well. They will gather up lots of data in order to keep up with the demands of their customers, which are always changing. The information that these retailers are able to collect and analyze can make it easier to identify some trends, recommend the right products, and overall help to increase the profits of that company.

These are just a few of the companies that are going to benefit from working with data analytics to help them out. There are a lot of different methods and techniques that we are able to use to make this work. But when we are able to put the parts together, and we make sure that we have the right types of data, we will be able to handle all of this and get some of the best insights to steer our predictions in no time.

Chapter 2: Reasons to Work with a Data Analysis

Now that we know a little bit more about working with data analysis and why this is such a good thing to work with overall, it is time for us to take a look at why a company would want to work with a data analysis overall. It is not the process that many companies are used to working with. When we learn how to make it work, though, and see some of the benefits that we are able to get out of it, we will find that it is an amazing option to handle as well.

Data is going to be available through a lot of different options. We can look at data through mobile app usage, digital clicks, interactions that happen on social media, and so more. This is all going to contribute to a unique data fingerprint that is going to be just their owner. Companies have to be able to learn the best way to take advantage of all of this to provide the customers with the kind of experience that the customer is looking for.

At the same time, companies are also finding that it is good for them to be more aware that creating the most engaging experience for the customer is going to provide them with some of the competitive advantages that they need. When we work with some advanced analytics, companies re able to make better use of their user and customer experience data. And this is going to lead to a lot of higher satisfaction and loyalty with the customers over time.

The good news is that there are a few benefits that any company will be able to experience when they use this data analysis. It is such a beneficial process, even though it can take some time, that it is definitely worth your time to learn more about how this works and what you are able to do with it. Some of the benefits that we are going to be able to notice when it comes to working with a data analysis includes

1. It can deliver the right products.

One of the ways that you are able to make some money for your business is to sell products and services. And with all of the competition that is out there, you need to make sure that you are releasing the right kinds of products in order to get started. There are other competitors out there, and customers sometimes don't realize what products they would most like. For example, if you bring out a new product like Amazon has done several times with products in the past like the Kindle, you need to be innovative and figure out what the customer would like before they even know.

Effective data collection, along with some good analytics, is going to make sure that a company is able to stay as competitive as possible. This can be especially important at any time that there is a newly developed technology or the customers come in with changes to their demands. This is also a good way to anticipate the demands of the market in order to provide the right products before they are even requested in the long run.

2. Personalization and service

With all of the competition out there, it is important that we are able to go through and provide something that is unique to our customers. It is too easy to get complacent, but we have to remember that there are a lot of different businesses out there who are able and willing to reach the niche of customers if you won't. And one of the best ways that you are able to really provide the best to the customers and get them to notice you some more, at least more than the competition, is to add in some personalize and service that others are not providing.

Companies have to be good and responsive in order to cope with a lot of the volatility that is created by their customers, especially the ones that are going to engage through some of the different digital technologies today. Being able to react in a manner that is more real-time, and can make the customer feel that your company really values them in a personal manner is going to be possible, but we have to make sure that we do this through advanced analytics.

Big data is going to help us gain the opportunity to interact with others based on the personality of that individual customer. It is going to help us do this by understanding more about the attitudes of the customer and then will consider some of the other factors, including real-time location, to help us deliver some personalization in a service environment that may rely on a bunch of different channels as well.

3. Helps us to be proactive and anticipate the needs of customers

Another reason that we would want to work with data analysis is that it is going to help us be more proactive when it comes to anticipating the needs of our customers. By sharing their own data with businesses, customers are going to expect that these companies know them a lot better. They expect to see relevant interaction and get a seamless experience across all of the touchpoints. This is something that your company is going to need to work in order to attract more customers in the future.

When you are able to go through and understand the needs of the customers, you will find that it is a lot easier to keep and maintain your customers as well. Companies are able to use this in order to understand the needs of their customers and then can optimize the customer experience, resulting in relationships that are strong and longstanding.

4. Optimize and then improve operational efficiency

When it comes to how well your business is able to perform, and the amount of money and time you are wasting, we want to make sure that we can keep this number down as much as possible. This is the best way to ensure that we can provide a good product to the customer and that we will be able to get them interested in sticking around. If we are not optimized as much as possible, then unnecessary costs are going to add up, and we may never get a chance to grow and do well because our product will be too expensive to work with.

Applying analytics for designing and controlling the process, and then doing what you can to optimize the operations of your business is going to ensure the efficiency and effectiveness so that we can fulfill the expectations of the customer, while still achieving some operational excellence in the process.

There are a number of ways that we are able to get this done. For example, it is possible for a business to work with a number of advanced analytics techniques so that they can improve their own productivity, efficiency, and field operations. And this is also a method that we can work with to figure out the best way to optimize the workforce of the customer based on the demands of the customers and their business needs.

If you are able to do a little bit of work and really optimize your business, and ensure that you are operating in a manner that reaches all of the demand of the customer without wasting money and having too much going on that doesn't need to be there, then your business is going to be more efficient. You will only spend money when it is needed, and this can help you to really get some great results in the process.

5. Mitigating risk and fraud

As a business, these are going to be two big things that we need to focus our time on. The more risk that your company takes on, the harder it is going to be to keep making money. A bit of risk is going to be fine and a normal part of running a business (though data analysis can help you to reduce the amount of risk that you are dealing with), but you never want to take on too much risk, or you will run your business into the ground.

Another thing to worry about, especially if you are in the financial industry, is the idea of fraud. When people try to commit fraud, it is going to harm the business and their other customers as well. Fraud has been responsible for millions of lost dollars over the years, so it makes sense that we would want to work with data analytics in order to reduce the amount of fraud that is going on and what we would like to do with it.

Security and fraud analytics, which can be done with data analysis, are going to aim to help us protect all of the intellectual, financial, and physical assets from being misused by any kind of internal and external threats. Efficient data and efficient analytics working together will be able to deliver what we need when it comes to optimum levels of fraud prevention and overall organizational security.

Data management is going to be a big part of all of this, and when we are able to use that management along with some efficient and transparent reporting of incidents of fraud along the way, this is going to help us get the improved fraud risk management processes that we want. In addition, when we are able to integrate and correlate all of our data throughout the whole business, no matter how big or small it is, we are able to offer a new and unified view of how fraud happens in the business based on the different lines of the business, the transactions, and the products at hand.

These are just a few of the different options that we are able to work with when it is time to handle data analysis. And no matter what kind of business you are in the first place, all five of the benefits above are going to be important to helping you to get things done while ensuring that you are offering a high-quality product to your customers in a timely and cost-effective manner.

There are other methods that you are able to utilize to help you to make plans for your business and to make it easier to come up with big decisions while reaching your customers and releasing products that they want. But none are going to be as effective as what we are going to see when we work with data analysis. That is why we are going to spend some time in this guidebook learning more about the different parts of Data analysis, how we can work with the Python language to make it more efficient, and so much more.

Chapter 3: How Does Python Fit Into This?

The next thing on our list that we need to focus on is how we can work with Python in order to complete the data analysis that we would like. There are a lot of different parts that come with our data analysis, and having it all come together, is going to take us some time and some good planning in the process. At one point, though, we will need to go through and make sure that we are working with a programming language, one that is versatile and strong, and one that is going to help us to run our algorithms as we go.

Our algorithms are very important to how well the data analysis will work. These are the pars that will take ahold of our data, and look through it all, sorting it through and telling us the insights or the patterns that are inside of it. But to get these to work well and to make sure that we are not going to end up with a big mess in the end and inaccurate results, we need to make sure that we are choosing a good and a strong language to get it done.

There are a lot of different coding languages that we are able to work with, and each one is going to bring about its own positives and negatives that we need to deal with. If you hear about the idea of coding and learning how to do a programming language, and it makes you nervous and anxious, have no fear. There are a lot of different languages that we are able to focus on in order to help us to handle our algorithms and get the best results when we want to work with our data analysis.

The number one language that is going to work for data analysis, and the machine learning that we need to accomplish in order to handle these algorithms, is

Python. As we are going to explore in this chapter, there are a lot of benefits that come with using Python, whether you just want to learn the basics of coding, or you are interested in handling something as complicated at data analysis. Let's dive in and see what some of these benefits are all about.

Python is an easy language to work with. If you are someone who has never done anything with coding before, and you are a bit nervous about getting started, and what that will be like, then the Python language is going to be one of the best options to help you get it off to a good start.

There are many options in coding languages out there, but a lot of them are going to be kind of difficult to learn. They are often reserved for some of the more complicated types of coding that you want to use, and you can build them later. But if you are a complete beginner in coding, then Python is going to be the best option for you. It is simple to read and use, and we will look at a few codes in the next chapter to help show how this is going to work for us. This can take some of the stress out of the whole process as well when it is time to learn a brand new coding language to work with data analysis.

Python has a large library that makes learning the codes easier. You will be amazed at how much power is going to be found when you work with Python, and how many options and functions are found in this language as well. whether you are a beginner or looking to add a few other parts and coding languages to your skill set, you will find that the traditional Python library is going to have all of the parts that you need to be more successful with it.

There are a lot of extensions and other libraries that work with Python that are specifically designed to enhance its capabilities and make it work better for a good data analysis. Even though the traditional library that comes with Python is going to include a lot of the power and more that you want with coding, there are other extensions that make sure you are able to complete some of the processes that you want with data science, data analysis, and even machine learning. Python, more than any other language, has a lot of these options, which can make it so much easier overall to get your work done.

There is a lot of power that you are able to enjoy when it is time to work on Python. Even though we have spent some time talking about how easy the Python language is going to be to learn, we have to remember that ease of use does not mean that you are missing out on power. The good news is that Python is going to come with a lot of power, and you will be able to use it in order to handle almost any project that you would like along the way.

The community of Python is going to be large, allowing even a beginner to get some of the assistance that they need along the way. This may not seem like a big deal, but when you are working on learning how to work with a new language, it is going to prove to be invaluable. Any time that you need to learn something new that you have a new question, or you get stuck, and you are not able to figure out how to get things fixed and working again, that community is going to be the answer that you need.

The community is going to include programmers from all around the world. And often, they will have a lot of different experience levels when it comes to how much they know how to do with coding. As a beginner, you can easily join and be included. And there are many programmers who are more advanced who are willing to share some of their time and knowledge with you as well. This helps to facilitate some of the work that you want to accomplish and can make it easier to learn something new.

You can use Python with some of the other languages that are sometimes a necessity when working with data analysis. For the most part, Python is going to work just fine with some of the work that you want to do with sorting, organizing, fixing, testing, training, and creating with data analysis. But there are a few algorithms that are going to perform a bit better when we work with some other coding languages.

The neat thing is that you can often use some of the libraries and extensions that come with Python to help fix this issue. You can write out the codes in the Python language, keeping it as easy and simple as possible, and then the extension is going to come in and take over, converting the language over to something else, and then executing it all for you. It is as simple as that for you to continue using the Python language in the way that you would like and still get the work done that is necessary.

Python works really well when it comes to handling some machine learning, which is often the core component that we see with the algorithms that run data analysis. While the focus of this guidebook is more about the basics of Python and of data analysis, we will find that when it comes to working on the algorithms that we want to handle in all of this, they are going to be run through the use of machine learning.

Machine learning is simply a process that helps take a program or even a whole system and set it up so that it is able to run on its own. The programmer will not have to come in and figure out all of the ways the system should behave. The system will be able to take the information that it gathers, and what it learns from the user, and use that to become smarter and better at its job overall. It is the main technology that is going to help us to run our algorithms so we can learn the patterns and insights that are needed in data analysis.

And the main language that is used to help create some of these machine learning algorithms in Python. Python can be used for other parts of the data analysis process, but you will also find that it is useful for helping us to create, train, and test the algorithms, ensuring that they are going to behave in the proper manner as well.

As we can see, there are a lot of different benefits that you will be able to enjoy when it comes to using Python. You can enjoy Python whether you are looking to increase some of your own knowledge base of programming and more, or if you are just looking for something to add to your skill sets. But it also works well for things like machine learning and data analysis, which are all going to be combined together for many of the projects that we want.

There may be a few other languages out there that we are able to work with that can handle our algorithms and may have some extensions and libraries that work with them to get the work done. But none are going to be as easy to use, as efficient to work with or provide the benefits that we are looking for, as we are able to find with the Python language. If you are looking for something that is simple to work with and will provide you with all of the benefits of learning how to program without taking years or months to figure out, then Python is the right one to use.

Don't worry if you have never done anything with coding in the past, though. Not only are we spending this chapter talking about how Python is beneficial as a coding language to learn, and how it is able to help us with some of the work that we want to do with data analysis, you will also find that it is going to be easy to learn. And the next chapter is going to take a look at some of the basics that you need to know in order to get started with coding in Python and making this work for your coding needs.

Chapter 4: Some of the Basic Codes in Python

Now that we have had a chance to look at Python and some of the benefits that come with it to ensure we get the full reasons why someone would want to use it for data analysis, it is time for us to go through some of the basics of writing code in Python. There are a lot of different parts that are all going to come together to help us make sure that we are writing our codes out well, and that we actually learn what Python is all about. That is why we are going to take some time to explore these in this chapter so we can use them later on in our data analysis.

Some of the different parts that you need to know when it comes to writing out codes in Python include:

The Keywords

The first part that we need to take a look at in here is the keywords. These are going to be special words, ones that are reserved, to help make sure that the compiler knows what commands it is supposed to follow along the way. There are a number of keywords that we are able to work within Python, and if we do not use them in the proper manner. If we go through and use the keywords at the wrong place, then you will end up with errors in your code, and it will not behave properly. But when this is done in the right location, then the compiler will know exactly what you are trying to get it to do.

Python Comments

The next thing that we need to take a look at in the comments. These are going to be unique parts of any code that allow you to add in a little bit of a note or information into the code without it actually affecting the code or causing it to have an error.

If you would like to name a certain part of the code, or you want to leave a little message for yourself, or for another programmer who would take a look through your information and your code. You can explain what is going through that part of the code for yourself or someone else, get it a different name, or something else.

Working on the comments is going to be simple to work with. Each code is going to work with these comments in a slightly different manner, but in the Python language, we just need to use the # symbol ahead of the comment. You can have the comment be as long or short as you would like, and you can have as many of these in your code as you would like as well. The rule is to just keep this to a minimum as much as possible, though, to ensure the code stays nice and clean along the way.

Python as an OOP Language

One thing that is unique about the Python language, along with a few others that are similar to it, is that this language is considered an object-oriented programming language, or OOP. This is going to be useful for you as a beginner because it ensures that your codes stay nice and organized along the way, and will make it easier for us to ensure the codes are going to behave in the way that we want them to.

Basically, this means that Python is going to be divided up into classes and objects to add to some organizations. The classes will be like containers in the code, there to help hold onto other parts that are similar to one another, or belong with one another in the code. You can add in as many of these classes as you would like along the way to help organize your objects, and we will take a look at some of the different ways that you can create these classes as well.

Then we can move on to the objects. The objects are going to be anything that we can place into the classes that we created. They will correspond to real objects that we find out in the world, so we won't have to deal with a bunch of abstract ideas along the way either. We will create the class that we want and then add in the objects to keep them together until they are called.

We are able to put in any kind of objects that we want into a class, as long as it makes sense for that object to be there. If someone else takes a look at the class that we work with, and they look at the objects, they should be able to tell why those specific objects are in the class together.

This doesn't mean that the objects in a class have to be identical to one another. But it should make sense why one object goes into that class, and another would not be put in. For example, you can have a class that includes farm animals and then add in as many of these animals as you want. You are not restricted to just putting spotted cows in a class.

How to Write a Class

The next thing that we need to take a look at here is how to write out some of our own classes in Python. Python is considered an object-oriented programming language, as we talked about above. Almost everything that we work within Python is going to be an object with the right methods and properties in place. A class is going to be like a blueprint or an object constructor that we are able to use when it is time to create the objects that we want to work with.

The good news is that creating a new class is not something that has to be all that difficult. We can create a simple class, and all that we need for this is the keyword of class. The code that we can use for this one includes:

```
class MyClass:
  x = 5
```

Once the class is done and created, we then need to go through and actually create an object that we are able to add to what we would like to have into that class. We are going to use the class that we created above, which is now known as myClass, to help us create objects. And we are able to do this with the following code:

```
p1 = MyClass()
print(p1.x)
```

While we are here, we are going to take a look at another function that we are able to introduce to our class that can make it work out better than it would on its own. The examples that we used above are going to be the classes and objects as we can use them in Python, but they are still in a pretty simple form and are not going to be that useful in most of the forms that we want to write out.

To help us get a better understanding of the meaning of these classes and what we are able to do with them, we need to understand one of the functions that have been built-in with Python, and that is the function of __init__().

All classes are going to have this function. This is because it is going to be important to help us get things done. This particular function is going to be executed as soon as we start to initiate the class as well.

We want to be able to work with this function in order to help assign some values to the properties of our objects, or to other operations that are necessary to do when we try to create the object. In the code that we are going to have below, we are going to create a class that we will name as Person, and then we will use the function above that we have been talking about to help us assign the values necessary for name and age:

```
class Person:
  def __init__(self, name, age):
    self.name = name
    self.age = age

p1 = Person("John", 36)

print(p1.name)
print(p1.age)
```

The next thing on the list that we need to explore is the object methods. These will be a bit different than the objects that we talked about above, but they are still important for us to spend some time on when we want to create our codes.

Objects can work on their own, or we can use them and make sure they contain methods. Methods are going to be found in objects, and this is when they are going to specifically be a function that will belong back to the object.

Now we are going to work on creating one of these object methods in that Person class we had before. We will also go through and insert a function that will print out a greeting for us and then execute it on the p1 object below:

```
class Person:
  def __init__(self, name, age):
    self.name = name
    self.age = age

  def myfunc(self):
    print("Hello my name is " + self.name)

p1 = Person("John", 36)
p1.myfunc()
```

and finally, we need to look at what is known as the self parameter. There are a lot of times when the parameter is going to be important to the code that we want to write out on a regular basis, and working with this specific parameter is going to be useful in a lot of the codes that we want to create.

To start, the "self" parameter is going to be a good reference that we can use to the current instance of our class. It is also going to be used to help access some of the variables that will belong to the class.

Of course, keep in mind here that we do not need to name this parameter as "self" to make it work. You are able to go through and give it any kind of name that you would like along the way. Just remember for it to work, it has to come in as the first parameter of any function that is found in your class. A good example of how to work with this particular type of parameter includes

```
class Person:
  def __init__(mysillyobject, name, age):
    mysillyobject.name = name
    mysillyobject.age = age
```

```
def myfunc(abc):
  print("Hello my name is " + abc.name)

p1 = Person("John", 36)
p1.myfunc()
```

Python Functions

Now that we have a better idea of how the classes are going to work in Python and why these are so important to some of the work that we want to create in this language, it is time to move on to some of the other parts of coding that are important for our goals as well. in particular, we are going to spend a bit of time looking at the steps that we are able to follow in order to create a function in the Python language.

A function, to start with, is just going to be a block of code, any block of code, which is only going to run when the compiler calls it out. You are able to pass on data, which will be known as a parameter, over to your function to ensure that it is going to work in the manner that you want. And then, as the function continues to do its job, it is able to return data as a result as well.

With this in mind, we need to take a look at some of the steps that we are able to use in order to create and then call one of the functions that we want to work with. This is fairly simple because we are able to define one of these functions with the use of the def keyword. The code that you can use to create one of these functions includes:

```
def my_function():
  print("Hello from a function")
```

Once the function is created and ready to go, it is then time for us to go through and call up a function. To call this function, we need to make sure that we rely on the name of the function (whichever name we decided to give to the function), and put it all into parenthesis. The code that we are able to use for this one will be below:

```python
def my_function():
    print("Hello from a function")
```

my_function()

While we are here, we need to take a closer look at something that is known as the arguments that come with functions. Some of the information that we pass over to the functions can be done more like an argument instead. Arguments are going to be specified after the name of the function, inside of our parenthesis to make sure that things are organized and ready to go. You are able to add in as many of these arguments as you would like, we just need to make sure that they have been separated out with a comma.

Now it is time for us to go through and see a good example of how this is going to work. The code that we will focus on here is going to have a function that just has one argument, which is known as (fname) when we are able to call up the function, we will pass along the first name, which is the going to be used inside of the function to help us get the full name printed off as well. The way that we would write out this code is below:

```
def my_function(fname):
  print(fname + " Refsnes")

my_function("Emil")
my_function("Tobias")
my_function("Linus")
```

now that we have brought up both the idea of a parameter and that of an argument, we need to figure out which one is going to be the best one to use for our codes. The terms of argument and parameter can be used for the same thing because both of them are going to include information that is passed on over to the function.

When we look at this from the perspective of the function, the parameter is going to be a variable that is listed inside of the parentheses in the definition of the function. The argument, on the other hand, is going to be the value that has been sent to the function when it is called out. We can use both in a similar manner along the way, though.

We can also work with the idea that is known as recursion. Python is also going to accept what is known as function recursion, which means that the defined function is able to come through and call itself.

Recursion is going to be a common concept in programming and mathematics. It means that a function is going to call itself. This has the benefit of allowing programming to loop through the data to reach the result that we are working with.

If you want to work with recursion, you need to be careful with the work that you handle here. It is easy to mess up and start writing a function that is never going to terminate, or one that is going to use too much memory or processing power to get the work done. However, when it is written out in the correct manner, it is possible for recursion to be efficient, and an elegant approach, mathematically, when you do your programming.

We are going to take a look at how to work with recursion below. This will make it easier for a beginner to get started learning how this works without having to worry as much about whether it is all going to work out well or not. The coding that we can use for this kind of recursion includes:

```
def tri_recursion(k):
  if(k>0):
    result = k+tri_recursion(k-1)
    print(result)
  else:
    result = 0
  return result

print("\n\nRecursion Example Results")
tri_recursion(6)
```

Python Variables

Now it is time for us to move on and take a look at how we are able to create some of the variables in our code, and why these are so important to coding in Python as well. Python variables are a simple idea. They are set up in order t hold onto a small spot in the memory of our computer as well. then we can assign a value over to it, just using an equal sign, so that something is actually held in the space of memory.

Variables are going to be containers that we can use to store the values of data. Unlike some of the other programming languages that you may use in the past, Python is not going to come with a command that will declare that variable for you. Instead, the variable is going to just be created the moment that you first give value over to it. A good example of how the code will look when you assign a value over to it is below:

```
x = 5
y = "John"
print(x)
print(y)
```

Variables do not need to have any declaration, and they don't have to be associated back to any particular type. We are even able to go through and change the type after we set them up. They are a lot easier to work with than what we may see in some of the other options of coding out there.

There will be a few rules that we have to keep in place when it is time to name the variable we want to use. You can make it easy and give the variable a short name, or you can go through and give it a name that is more descriptive of what it is holding onto. Some of the rules that we are able to utilize when it comes to our Python variables will include:

1. The name of the variable has to start with a letter or the underscore character.
2. A variable name is not allowed to start with a number.
3. A variable name can only contain things like alpha-numeric characters and the underscore, so nothing special in there.
4. The name recognizes case sensitivity. This means that there will be a difference between BLUE, Blue, and blue in this language.

Lists vs. Dictionaries

Another topic that is going to show up when we work with Python is the differences between a list and a dictionary, and even a tuple. First, we are going to explore what the lists are like. The list is going to actually have the most versatility when it comes to types of objects that are used in Python. Some of the things that we will notice when working on these lists include

1. A list is going to be an ordered and mutable sequence of items. Because of this, it is something that we are able to slice, index, and change along the way. Each element is something that we are able to access using the position it has on the list. Python lists are going to work for most of the collection data structures, and since they are found as built-in, you do not have to go through the process of manually creating them.
2. Lists are going to be used for any object type, from strings to numbers and to more lists as well.
3. They are going to be accessed just like a string, which means that they are simple to use, and they will be variable in length. We are able to

see them shrink and grow automatically as we use them.

4. List variables are going to be declared when we work with the brackets, and then the name of the variable will be ahead of it.

Another option to explore is known as a tuple. Tuples are going to be used in Python to help hold together more than one object. Think of this as something that is similar to the list, but it is not going to have the extensive functionality that the list class is going to provide to us. One of the major features that we will like about these tuples is that they are going to be immutable, similar to strings, which means we are not able to modify them.

Even though modification is not allowed here, you are able to take portions of some of the existing tuples and use it to make a new tuple. Lists are going to be declared with a square bracket, and then we are able to change them as needed. However, the tuple is going to be found in the parentheses, and we are not able to change them at all.

And third on the list in the dictionary. This one is a bit unique in Python as well because it is going to focus on things in a different manner. The dictionary is going to rely mostly on what is known as the key: value pair, which is similar to what we would know as an associative array if you have worked in other programming languages.

A good way to think about the dictionary is like an address book where we are going to be able to find the address or the contact details of a person simply by knowing their name. With the dictionary, we are going to associate the keys or the name, with the values, or the details, to get what we want in the process. We must note here, though, that the key has to be unique for this to work, similar to how we are not able to find the right information on a person if we have two individuals with the same name.

Creating a Simple Loop

There are actually a few different types of loops that we are able to work with when it comes to Python. These are going to be nice because they take out some of the work. If there is a part of the code that you would like to see repeat itself a bunch of times, rather than rewriting out that part of code over and over again, we would simply turn it into a loop. In specific, we are going to take a look at what the for loop is about and how we can utilize this for our needs too.

To start, the for loop is going to be used to help us iterate over one of the sequences that we want to use. This could be a string, a set, a dictionary, a tuple, or a list. This is going to be less like the keyword that we see with other coding languages, and it is more like the iterator method for other OOP languages.

When we focus on the for loop, we are going to spend some time executing a set of specific statements that we want to see taken care of. This is going to happen one time for each item on the list, tuple, or set. A good example that we can look at here is below:

```
fruits = ["apple", "banana", "cherry"]
for x in fruits:
  print(x)
```

Now in some cases, we also have to make sure that we add in a break statement. This will ensure that the code will know where to stop and that it is not going to keep going in an endless loop that we are not able to stop. This will effectively freeze up our computers and make it hard to work with them without exiting the whole program. Set up the broken part in this to ensure that it will behave in the manner that you want.

The If Else Statement in Decision Control

There will be some situations where you will want to let the computer make a decision on its own. This will often be a decision that is based on the input that the user provides to the computer. You can set up some conditions to tell the computer how to behave, or the program how to behave. But since you are not able to guess all of the potential inputs that the user is going to work with, we need to work with what is known as the decision control statements.

There are three main ones in the Python language. There is the if statement, the if else statement, and the elif statement. All of these are going to work in slightly different manners and can be important based on the information that we want to include in our statements. But we are going to spend our time here looking at the method that is used the most in these decision control statements, and that is the if else statement.

This statement is going to have at least two possible outcomes. If the input from the user is true based on the conditions that you set, then the if part of the statement is going to be applied and executed. If the input of the user is not true based on the conditions that you set, then the computer is going to execute the else statement.

We can also go down the line with this one a few times and have a few different if statements. Then the program is going to just check each one and determine if the input is true based on that condition. If it is, then that is the statement that the compiler will execute. If it is not, then it goes all the way down the line until it reaches the else statement, and that will be the one that is executed.

The syntax that we are able to use for this one will be below


```
if expression:
   statement(s)
else:
   statement(s)
```

The cool thing here is that we are able to take this one a bit further if we would like. A good example of how to write out some codes that work with our if else statement would be the two options below:

```python
#!/usr/bin/python

var1 = 100
if var1:
   print "1 - Got a true expression value"
   print var1
else:
   print "1 - Got a false expression value"
   print var1

var2 = 0
if var2:
   print "2 - Got a true expression value"
   print var2
else:
   print "2 - Got a false expression value"
   print var2

print "Goodbye!"
```

Can I Create an Inheritance?

The final thing that we are going to look at in this part about Python and how to handle it is the inheritance in Python. Inheritances in Python will allow us to define a class that is able to inherit all of the properties and the methods from the class that we created in the past already. There are two main parts that come with the inheritance, and these include the parent class and the child class.

The parent class is going to be the original class or the one that is being inherited from. You will sometimes see that it is called the base class. Then there is the child class. This is going to be the class we work with that will inherit from another class. We can sometimes call it the derived class.

With this in mind, we are going to take a look at some of the steps that we can use in order to create our own parent class. Any class can technically be one of these parent classes. Because of this, the syntax that you are going to use is similar to what we talked about earlier when we created just a simple class. The code that you can use includes:

```python
class Person:
  def __init__(self, fname, lname):
    self.firstname = fname
    self.lastname = lname

  def printname(self):
    print(self.firstname, self.lastname)

#Use the Person class to create an object and then execute the printname method:

x = Person("John", "Doe")
x.printname()
```

Now that we have gone through and created the parent class and we have that all set up, it is time for us to go through and create the child class that we want to work with. This is going to be the class that takes things from the original parent class and makes it unique and new. We can take things away and add in more without messing with the parent class at all, but we will still use some of the basis of the parent class here.

Now we want to go through the process of creating that child class. To help us create a class that is able to handle and inherit the functionality from another class, we want to make sure that we send the parent class as the parameter we want to use when creating the child class. The code that we are able to use to make this happen includes:

```
class Student(Person):
  pass
```

Remember that __init__() function that we talked about earlier? We need to bring that back in here to help us out. In the codes above, we have simply created a child class that is going to inherit all of the methods and properties from the original code. We want to bring in this function to the child class rather than working with the pass keyword because this function is going to be called any time that we want to use the class to create a new object. This will just make it all easier down the line. The code that we want to use to make this happen includes:

```
class Student(Person):
  def __init__(self, fname, lname):
    #add properties etc.
```

At some point, we are going to want to add some properties to the child class. This allows us to not just work with the exact code that we had before. But we will be able to go through and make some of the changes to this new child code as some of the functionality of the parent code, but there will be some differences as well so that we can have it be brand new and working for or needs. The code that we can use when we would like to add in some properties to our child class includes:

```python
class Student(Person):
  def __init__(self, fname, lname):
    super().__init__(fname, lname)
    self.graduationyear = 2019
```

in addition to working with the properties that we want to add into the code, we need to go through and add in some of the right methods as well. these are slightly different, but we are able to work with it to help our child class act in the manner that we want. The example that we are going to take a look at below will add in a method that we will name as "welcome" to the class that is labeled as "Student". The code that we want to take a look at to make this happen is below:

```python
class Student(Person):
  def __init__(self, fname, lname, year):
    super().__init__(fname, lname)
    self.graduationyear = year

  def welcome(self):
    print("Welcome", self.firstname, self.lastname, "to the class of", self.graduationyear)
```

If you go through and add in a method that goes to your child class with the same name as a function in the parent class, you have to note that the inheritance of that parenting method is going to be overridden, so keep that in mind when you get started.

As we can see, there are a lot of different parts that are going to come into play when we are working with the Python language. And all of these codes can help you to learn more about how this language works, and what we are able to do with it overall. After you get some practice with this, you will be ready to go if you decide to work with data analysis, and you get ready to create your own algorithms to make this happen.

Chapter 5:
What is the NumPy Library

Now it is time for us to take a look at one of the great libraries that we can work with when it comes to using Python and getting our data analysis to work well for our needs. NumPy is one of the first that we can look at, and it is going to be one of the best. It is actually going to be the basis that we can see with some of the other important libraries that we will discuss later on, or other data analysis libraries, so it is worth our time to take a look at it.

To start with, NumPy is a library that is used in Python. We are able to use it for a number of different reasons, including numerical as well as scientific computing if we need it. For the most part, though, it is going to be used to help us compute our array s in a quick and efficient manner. We will have it based and written out in the Python and the C language.

Even though this is a language that works for the C language as well, this is going to be a basic data analysis library that we are going to use with Python, and the word NumPy is going to stand for Numerical Python. We are going to bring out this library to help us to process any of the homogeneous multidimensional arrays that we want to handle.

This library is going to be one of the core libraries that is used for different scientific computations. This means that it is going to have a powerful array of objects that are multidimensional, and it will integrate some tools that are useful when it is time to really work with these arrays as well.

You will quickly find that when you work with the data analysis that we have been talking about that NumPy is going to be useful in almost all of the scientific programming that we try to do with Python, including things like statistics, machine learning, and bioinformatics. It is also going to provide us with some good functionality that we are able to work with, functionality that is able to work well will run in an efficient manner, and is well written in the process.

As we mentioned before, this is going to be a library that is focused mainly on performing some of the mathematical operations that we need to use on contiguous arrays, much like the arrays that are found in a few other languages, including what is seen in the C language. This means that we are able to use NumPy to help us manipulate some of our numerical data as well

Understanding More About NumPy

You will quickly find that outside of the standard Python library. The NumPy library is going to be one of the most used libraries in Python. Data science techniques and algorithms of all kinds are going to need work to be done by the matrices, large size arrays, and lots of numerical computation in order to look through their data and learn what is there. And NumPy is going to be able to take on this job in a seamless manner.

This library is really basic, but it is still going to be important when it comes to handling some of the scientific computing that we want to do with Python. Plus, it will not take that long working with data science and data analysis before you find that this is going to be the library that other data analysis libraries are going to be dependent on.

Some of the other major libraries are going to be dependent on the arrays in NumPy as their inputs and outputs. In addition to this, it is also going to provide some functions that are going to allow developers a way for developers to perform all of the basic and the advanced functions that they would like, whether we are talking about statistics or mathematics, especially when we are dealing with multi-dimensional arrays and matrices, without needing to use as many lines of codes to get it all done.

When we compare these arrays with the lists that we talked about earlier with Python, you will find that the arrays are going to be much faster. But Python lists do have an advantage over the arrays because they are more flexible as you are only able to store the same data type in each column when we are working with the arrays.

There are a few features that you are going to enjoy when it is time to work with the NumPy library. Some of the main features that you will enjoy the most will include:

1. The NumPy library is going to be a combination of Python and C language,
2. This is going to consist of arrays that are homogeneous and multi-dimensional.

Ndarray is part of this as well, which will be n-dimensional arrays as well.

3. It is going to work on a lot of different functions for arrays if you would like.
4. It can also help us to reshape the arrays. It also allows Python to have a way to work as an alternative to MATLAB.

There are a lot of reasons why we would want to work with NumPy rather than having to pick one of the other libraries that are out there along the way. We will use the array in NumPy for the work that we are doing with Python instead of a list. And some of the reasons for this include it is convenient to work with, it is going to perform faster than other methods, and it is going to use less memory overall.

All of these are going to be important when we are trying to do some of the algorithms that we need in data analysis. And mostly, you will notice that the arrays are going to be the number one thing that we utilize when it is time to work with this library as well.

There are a few other things that we need to explore when it comes to how we are able to work with the NumPy library. First, the NumPy array is going to take up a lot less space than other options. The arrays that we have been talking about in this chapter are going to be a lot smaller when it comes to size than we will see with the lists in Python. A list with this language is able to take about 20MB of space, which is going to really take up space on your computer if you work with a few of these.

On the other hand, we are able to create an array, and it is only going to take about 4 MB. If you need to use a lot of different arrays as you go through, and they are going to fit better on the space of your memory overall. Arrays are also going to be easier to access when you would like to read and write on them later on.

In addition, the performance when it comes to speed, you will find that the NumPy arrays are going to be great. It is going to be able to perform a lot faster when it comes to computations than what we find with the Python lists. Because this library is considered open-sourced, it is not going to cost you anything to get started with. Then it also has the benefit of working with the popular Python programming language, which has high-quality libraries for almost all of the tasks that you want to accomplish.

All of these are great benefits to work with. You will find that it is a high-quality library that is going to help us to get things done. You can get it to match up with the libraries that you want, it is going to be free to work with, and it can handle a lot of the data analysis projects that you want to do. It is also an easy library that will connect some of the codes that are already existing in the C language over to the interpreter for Python so you can get your work done.

There are a lot of benefits that are going to come up when you want to work with the NumPy library, and you will find that it is going to be the basis for a lot of the codes and algorithms that you want to write out when you are working with your data analysis. Learning how to use this language and what it is able to do for you is going to make a world of difference in how much you are able to accomplish for the long-term, and it is worth your time to learn more about it as well to complete your project.

Chapter 6:
Taking It Further with Pandas

The next option that we need to take a look at is a bit of the work that we are able to do with the Pandas library. This is one of the most important libraries that we are able to work with overall because it is able to handle pretty much all of the parts that come with data analysis. There isn't anything in data analysis that the Pandas library won't be able to help us out with.

Pandas are going to be one of the packages from Python that is able to provide us with numerous different tools to help us with data analysis. The package is going to come with a lot of different structures of data that can be used for the different tasks that we need to do to manipulate our data. It is also going to come with a lot of methods that we are able to invoke for the analysis, which is going to be really useful when we are ready to work on some of our machine learning and data science projects in this language.

As we can imagine already, there are a number of benefits that we can enjoy when we work with the Pandas library, especially when compared to some of the other options out there. First, it is going to present for our data in a manner that is suitable to handle all of our analysis through the different data structures, in particular through the DataFrame and the Series structures.

In addition to this, we are going to find that this is a package that is able to contain a lot of different methods that are going to be convenient for data filtering and more. The Pandas library will come with a lot of the utilities that we need to perform operations of Input and Output in a manner that is seamless. And no matter which format your data is going to come to us in, whether it is CSV, MS Excel, or TSV, the Pandas library is going to be able to handle it for us.

How to Install Pandas

When you work with the traditional Python distribution, you will find that it is not going to have the module of Pandas. You will need to go through the process of installing this to your computer in order to get it to work. The nice thing that you will quickly notice, though, is that Python is going to come with a tool that is known as pip, which is exactly what you want to use in order to install Pandas on your own computer. In order to do this specific installation, we need to go through and use the command below:

$ pip install pandas

If you already have the Anaconda program on your system, then you need to use a slightly different command to help you out. This command is going to be:

```
$ conda install pandas
```

It is often recommended that when you do this process, you go through and install the latest version of the Pandas package to get all of the new features and more that we need along the way. However, it is still possible to get some of the older versions, and you can install this one as well. you can just go through and specify which of the versions that you would like to use when working on the conda install code that we did above.

The Data Structures in Pandas

With some of this in mind, it is time for us to go through a few of the different things that we are able to do with the Pandas code. First, we need to look at the data structures. There are two of these data structures that we are able to work with, including the series and the DataFrame.

The first one here is the series. This is going to be similar to what we are able to work with when it comes to a one-dimensional array. It is able to go through and store data of any type. The values of a Pandas Series are going to be mutable, but you will find that the size of our series is going to be immutable, and we are not able to change them later.

The first element in this series is going to be given an index of 0. Then the last element that is going to be found in this kind of index is N-1 because N is going to be the total number of elements that we put into our series. To create one of our own Series in Pandas, we need to first go through the process of importing the package of Pandas through the insert command of Python. The code that we are able to use, including:

Import pandas as pd

Then we can go through and create one of our own Series. We are going to invoke the method of pd.Series() and then pass on the array. This is simple to work with. The code that we are able to use to help us work with this includes:

Series1 = pd.Series([1, 2, 3, 4])

We need to then work with the print statement in order to display the contents of the Series. You can see that when you run this one, you have two columns. The first one is going to be the first one with numbers starting from the index of 0 like we talked about before, and then the second one is going to be the different elements that we added to our series. The first column is going to denote the indexes for the elements.

However, you could end up with an error if you are working with the display Series. The major cause of this error is that the Pandas library is going to take some time to look for the amount of information that is displayed, this means that you need to provide the sys output information. You are also able to go through this with the help of a NumPy array like we talked about earlier. This is why we need to make sure that when we are working with the Pandas library, we also go through and install and use the NumPy library as well.

The second type of data structure that we are able to work with here will include the DataFrames. These are going to often come in as a table. It is going to be able to organize the data into columns and rows, which is going to turn it into a two-dimensional data structure. This means that we have the potential to have columns that are of a different type, and the size of the DataFrame that we want to work with will be mutable, and then it can be modified.

To help us to work with this and create one of our own, we need to either go through and start out a new one from scratch, or we are going to convert other data structures, like the arrays for NumPy into the DataFrame.

There are a lot of different parts that we are able to handle when it comes to the Pandas library. And getting this set up and ready to go for some of our own needs is important in this process as well. this is one of the best libraries to work with when it is time to handle our work with Python coding with data analysis. This can handle all of the different parts that come with the data analysis along the way.

Chapter 7: The Importance of Cleaning and Organizing the Data

Now that we know a bit more about the data analysis and how it is going to work, and how to work with the Python language, it is time for us to work with the first steps that are necessary to handle this process. There are a number of steps that we need to focus on when it comes to handling the data. And this means that we are not going to start out with just creating our algorithms and calling it good. Instead, we need to do a bit of work to gather the data that we want to use, and then we need to be able to clean and organize it in a manner that it will be able to handle the analysis that we want to do.

In this chapter, we are going to take a look at some of the steps that we need to do in order to get started with our own data analysis. There are a few parts that come with this one including setting up our initial questions, looking at the right steps to help us collect the data, exploring how the data works, handling the outliers, and the missing values, along with the duplicates and more. Let's dive in a bit and look at some of the steps that belong to this part of the process.

Collecting the Data

The first step to this process is to actually gather the data that we want to handle. The good news here is that we have a lot of sources that we can use to find our data. We live in a world that has a ton of data right at our fingertips. From asking customers questions about their products, looking at some of the shopping habits of their customers, going through various websites, conducting websites, and more. There is a wealth of information that we are able to use on a regular basis, and learning how to find the data, and making sure that it is high quality so that we can use it correctly in our algorithms.

To start here, we need to have a good idea of what we are looking for when it comes to the data that we want to use. What is your goal in using this data? What are you hoping to accomplish when you have this data, and what is the point of working with the data analysis in the process? This is going to be important because it helps us to make sure that we are actually going to have everything in order and that we search through the right kind of data as we go.

Once we have our direction, it is time to start gathering up the data that you need to make this happen. There are a lot of sources that you are able to rely on based on what you are looking up. Social media is a good place to start. You can also work with online searches, third party surveys and research, focus groups, and more.

Gathering up a lot of data is important. But it is more important to make sure that your data is high-quality. The better the quality of your data, the more that it is going to be there to help our algorithms do well and ensure that we will be able to rely on the different results that we get. It is never a good idea to go through and just use any old data that you can find. This is going to make it impossible to get accurate results, and it will not be worth your time to do the data analysis in the first place.

Organizing the Data

Once we have had a chance to go through and collect all of the data that we need, it is time for us to go through and organize some of the data. If you get it from all of the different sources that we talked about before, it is likely that you will end up with a pretty good mess here. There is a lot of good data that you are able to go through and sort as you go. But it is going to come with missing and duplicate values, in a bunch of different formats, and there are likely to be a ton of outliers and other issues that we need to work with. This is going to make it hard for us to go through and know how to handle the data, and your algorithm will not be able to do anything about this until you can actually go through and organize it.

The first step that we need to work on here is making sure that we are able to get the data as organized as possible along the way. And a good first step here is to sort it out into a common format. Many businesses like to take their data and get it to fit into a spreadsheet or another similar format. This is going to help us to really keep things organized as we go, and can make it a lot easier for us to look it over and have it sorted.

Depending on the kind of data that we are working with, you may find that working with something else or another type of software that we are going to handle. You need to just make sure that the information ends up in the right format. The goal is to get the data to be in the same format so that it behaves and can all go through the different algorithms that you want to work with along the way. This can take some time, but it is going to make your life so much easier as you work through some of the steps that we will do along the way.

Dealing with the Outliers

Another thing that we need to work with here is the outliers. There are some situations where these are going to be useful and can help us to get a lot done and even sow off some new niches and ideas that we have not considered before, but other times, they are just going to be in the way and can skew your results away from some of the real options that you should consider.

In many cases, you will want to ignore the outliers and get rid of them. There will just be a few of them that are way off from the mean or the average that you want to use and can make your results go way over from what they should be. When you look at the data, or even a chart about the data, and you notice that it has just a few pieces or points that do not match up where they should, then it is best to just delete these so they don't mess with the results you should get.

On the other hand, it is always a good idea to take a closer look at the outliers because there are times when they will share important information with you. If you look at these outliers and see there are a number of these outliers that happen to all around the same area, then this could give you some information that can grow your business. It may show you a new niche or a new demographics that you are able to market to and work with.

Sometimes, your outliers are going to be important, so it is at least worth your time to take a look at them and see what you are able to learn. However, keep in mind that these outliers are not always going to matter, and in many cases, they are just going to mess with the results that you get out of your algorithms if you do not get rid of them. Check them out, but be ready to delete them and get rid of them to ensure that you can get accurate results later on.

Filling in Missing Data

There are times when we want to work with our data, and we will notice that there are data points that are missing. When we try to collect our data from a wide variety of sources, this is something that is likely to happen along the way. It is important for us to go through and decide what we want to do with these missing values so that they don't skew the rest of our data and cause issues.

There are a few different methods that we are able to use to make this one work for us. If there are only a few of these options in the data set, then they are probably not that big of a deal, and it is easiest for us to just delete those missing values and not deal with them.

The issue with this one, though, is that there are usually a significant number of values that are missing, or you do not want to delete things if you are just missing one thing in a collection for a customer and the rest of the information is there and can be useful. This is why we will usually need to manipulate the information a bit and see how we are able to make some changes to ensure that this is going to still work for us.

One of the methods that are popular to work with is to take the average of the other similar columns in your data. You can set it up so that if something is missing, have it set up so that you are able to fill it all in wit the average of the other columns. This is a quick and efficient manner of handling some of this information and will help to deal with some of the outliers that we are able to find in our data.

How to Deal with Duplicates

There are times when we are working through our data, and we will end up with a lot of duplicates. There are times when just a few of these are not going to be that big of a deal. But if we are going through and have quite of these duplicates, then there are going to be a few issues along the way. It is going to end up skewing some of the work that we do with the other data in the spreadsheet or the other source that we are working with.

Duplicates are not going to seem like a big issue as we go through the whole process of doing our data analysis. But you will find that if we are able to go through and get through the process of getting rid of the duplicates, then everything is going to work a bit better. Your results will show up in a more accurate manner, and you will be able to get everything to line up during the training and the testing phase as well.

This is why we need to take some time to go through all of our data and eliminate the duplicates as much as possible. You can decide, based on the types of data that you are working with, how many duplicates you will allow. Sometimes it is fine to have a few duplicates in the data, and it is not going to affect things too much. But if you end up with more than that, it is possible to see this happen, and you may not be able to trust your data. Then there are some people who will choose to go through and cut the duplicates down so there are no longer any of these in the data at all.

Cleaning the data that you will use in your own data analysis is something that takes some time. You will find that it actually will take up the most time of all the other processes that we need to handle in our data analysis. This is because the data analysis needs us to have data that is organized and easy to work with. If there are duplicates, missing data, and data that is not that organized, then you will find that the results that you get are not going to be that accurate along the way.

The more time that we are able to spend organizing and getting our data to be as high-quality as possible, the better. This helps to speed up the training and testing process of our algorithms later on and can make it so much easier for us to actually trust the results that we are able to get along the way. This is important if we actually want to use the data analysis to help us make some important and smart decisions along the way, and can ensure that we are able to get ahead of the competition and more. It may not be the most glamorous part of the whole process, but it is one of the most important parts.

Chapter 8: Training, Testing, and Repeating

Now that we have had a chance to spend time looking for the data that we want to use, and that we have had a chance to clean and organize all of our data, it is time to move on to the part that is a bit more fun in the process. It is time for us to look a bit more at the fun part. We are going to look at some of the fun things that we are able to do when it comes to our algorithms and making sure that they are able to provide us with some of the accurate results that we are able to handle with this.

There is actually a good deal of work that we need to do when it comes to working with our algorithms. You can't just push the data through and assume it is going to provide us with a few of the different options that we want along with the way. These algorithms are not going to be set up to provide us with accurate results right off the bat. We need to be able to go through and really look through, doing the training and the testing of the algorithms to help us increase the accuracy. When the accuracy is high enough, only then are we able to go through and really see some amazing results with our algorithms.

With this in mind, let's take a closer look at some of the steps that we need to take in order to get this done, and to ensure that we are able to really get these algorithms to work well in the long run.

Picking Out the Algorithms to Use

The first thing that we need to consider here is which of the different algorithms we are going to use. There are a number of algorithms that we are able to handle. And it is going to take some time to really ensure that we pick out the right one depending on the data that we want to work with, and the types of information that we are working with when it comes to our data.

There are a lot of algorithms that we are able to handle, and they are going to fall under three main styles of machine learning, which is the idea that is going to really push and run our algorithms. These are going to include supervised learning, unsupervised learning, and reinforcement learning.

We are going to explore these in more detail in the next chapter. But we can take a moment to look through these here as well. To start with, we have supervised learning. This is where we are going to show a lot of examples to the algorithm with the right answers to the end. This helps the program to learn from these examples. Then we are able to test it on the knowledge it learns as we go through this process.

Then it is time to work with unsupervised learning. This one is a bit different because we are not going to show the algorithm the results with the example that we use. We expect the program to be able to learn all on its own. Instead, we are going to take the time to have the program learn on its own. This takes a bit more time for the program to learn and gain the right accuracy that we want. But when it gets to this point, you will find that the unsupervised learning is going to be really strong and can take on a lot more options and program capabilities than we will be able to go with all of the other choices.

And then we can move on to what the reinforcement learning. This one is going to take us to another level as well, though, in the beginning, it is going to look like it is pretty much the same as the unsupervised learning that we were talking about above. The main difference that we are going to see with this one is that we will set this up in more of a trial and error kind of method.

Reinforcement learning is going to work on trial and error and will be able to learn when it does things wrong or gets the answer wrong. It will remember all of this and work from there in order to get more accuracy. It learns on its own but has a set of rewards and punishments to help reinforce the kind of learning that we are trying to work with.

All of these can be important in helping us to handle some of the different things that we want to do with our data analysis. Since all of them are different, though, we need to make sure that we are going through and choosing the one that will help us out with our needs.

Take your time when you pick out the algorithms that you want to work with. There are a ton of options, and all of them have benefits and some negatives that you need to work with as well. Learning about some of the different types and how they work will help us to really work through our data and find the results that we want.

Training Our Data

The next thing on the list that we need to explore is how to train our data. It would be nice to pick out the algorithm we want to run, throw the data into it, and then use the results that come out of that, knowing that they are accurate right from the beginning. But this is not the way things actually work. We need to take some time to work with that algorithm and train it to behave well.

This is where we will need to take all of that data that we found and worked through in the last chapter, and split it up. We need to have at least two categories here. We will have one to be in our training set and one that will be a part of our testing set. Each of these is going to have their own roles to follow and can be important to ensure that we are going to be able to teach our algorithms the proper way to behave.

First, we have the training data set. This is the set of data that we are going to use in order to make it easier to teach the algorithm how to behave. We will show the data with the corresponding right answers along with it. This needs to be the set of data that is the highest quality so that we can ensure that the algorithm is going to learn the right information along the way. Take your time to push the data through, maybe even doing it a few times so that the algorithm has more instances where it is able to learn how to behave in the process.

Testing the Data

After we have had some time to train our algorithm, and all of the training data has gone through that chosen algorithm, it is time to do some testing. Using a brand new set of data (remember that we split our data up into two parts in the beginning), we will push the data through the algorithm to see what results we can get.

The accuracy level that we end up with here is going to tell us a lot of information. For example, it is going to let us know whether the algorithm was able to learn along the way, how well it learned, and how much more work we need to do to make this process accurate enough that we are able to rely on it along the way with the data analysis.

When you do the testing part of the process, you want to aim to get above 50 percent. You do not need to get all the way in the 90 or even the 100 percentile, because this is going to happen with time, not with just one training and one testing session. Even if you get a number that is lower, like in the low 60 percent, then this is a good sign.

The assumption when you go through this is that any accuracy that is above 50 percent shows us that the algorithm was able to learn. We assume that even if the algorithm did not have any training at all, and we just jumped right in with the testing, the algorithm should be able to give us some results that are correct, at least half of the time. If you can get an accuracy that is above that, then this is a good sign that your training went well. You may need to go through it a few more times to get the accuracy up a bit more, but this is still a good sign.

If you do this, though and your accuracy ends up below 50 percent, then we have a problem. The algorithm should never get below this much accuracy, and if you are seeing these kinds of numbers, then it is likely that your training went wrong. These numbers are usually indicative of your data is bad, and that you did not get the high-quality data that you should have to start.

With these kinds of numbers, you need to go all the way back to the drawing board. Using the same kind of data to go through the process again is not going to do you or anyone else any good, and it can really cause some harm to the results that you get through this. It is probably best to go out and find some better data, data that is higher in quality. At the very least, you should take the time to rework on your data and make sure that it is going to behave in the manner. Whether this means better organization, checking the missing values, cleaning it more, or picking out a different algorithm, there is something that needs to change when this starts to happen to you.

Hopefully, we do not have that last problem, and instead, we end up with an algorithm that learned something. It may not be as high of accuracy as we would like to start with, but it can be a good start. We will need to go through the process and get it higher, but if you can get any accuracy that is above 50 percent, then pat yourself on the back because you have started off on the right foot in this process.

Repeat the Process

Unfortunately, this is not where it all ends. Unfortunately, getting 60 percent accuracy is not going to be an excuse to walk away and do nothing else with some of the work that you want to handle. It is a good start, but we need to rinse and repeat to get this higher. Our goal here is not to get it to 100 percent. That takes a long time and won't really happen until we put this into some of the real-world applications that we are hoping with these algorithms. However, if you are looking to use this as a way to make decisions and learn more about your industry, it is likely that you want the algorithm to start out with more accuracy than 60 percent.

So, how do we get the accuracy to be higher? We go through the same steps that we outlined above, many times over. When the first test is done, we go through and do another set of training, making sure that the data we rely on is strong and will provide us with the answers that we want. Then, when that training is all done, we go through and do another test, and hope that we are able to get a higher accuracy level in the process.

This is a process that we may have to repeat multiple times in order to get the accuracy that we want. The cool thing about machine learning, though, is that these algorithms are able to learn, and they will get better at some of the work they do. The more data that you feed to them, the more that they are able to learn from that information along the way. And as long as your training and testing data are higher in quality and are on the right topics, you will find that it is going to work in your favor, and the accuracy levels will go up.

The number of times that you need to go through this process will often depend on your own goals and what you are hoping to accomplish. If you want to get the accuracy level up as high as possible before you start working with the algorithm, then you will need to do more iterations of the training and the testing. If having a little bit lower accuracy is fine because you know the algorithm will have plenty of time to learn as it goes, then you may be able to get away with fewer iterations to get this done. It all depends on the kind of project that we are going in the first place.

Working with the different algorithms that are present in data analysis is kind of fun, and is one of the parts of the process that many people are excited to learn how to work with in the first place. When you get to this part, we are finally going through the steps to learn how to make the algorithms behave so that you can use them to make smart business decisions for your needs.

While this part is exciting, it is important to not get ahead of yourself too much here. You still need to take some precautions and think things through to ensure that you are doing it in the proper manner. If you rush through it, the accuracy is not going to be there, and you will not get the algorithms and more to behave in the manner that you would like.

However, this is going to be some of the fun stuff in the data analysis process, and you will quickly find as you work through these algorithms that this is exactly why we needed to take so much time to work on the data organization and cleaning that we talked about before. It will ensure that this part of the process stays fun and that you can actually get some of the accurate results that are so important here.

Chapter 9: Machine Learning and How It Fits Into Our Data Analysis

The next topic that we need to talk about when it comes to data analysis is machine learning. This is going to be an important part of our data analysis because it helps us to work with some of the algorithms and the models that we want to control in this process. With the help of machine learning and the use of the Python language that we talked about earlier, we are able to see our algorithms actually work and do some of the insights and predictions that we want to work with along the way.

To help us see why machine learning can be useful to our data analysis, we need to take a closer look at how machine learning is going to work in the first place.

This chapter is going to take a look at what machine learning is all about, what we can do with it, and some of the different types of machine learning that are important as we go through this.

What is Machine Learning?

The first thing that we need to take a look at here is the basics of machine learning. This is going to be one of the techniques that we can use with data analytics that will help teach a computer how to learn and react on their own, without the interaction of the programmer. Many of the actions that we will train the system to do will be similar to actions that already come naturally to humans, such as learning from experience.

The algorithms that come with machine learning are going to be able to use computational methods in order to learn information right from the data, without having to rely on an equation that is predetermined as its model. The algorithms are going to adaptively improve some of their own performance as the number of samples that we will use for learning will increase.

There are a lot of instances where we are able to use machine learning. With the rise in big data that is available for all industries to use, We will find that machine learning is going to become one of the big techniques that are used to solve a ton of problems in many areas, including the following:

1. Computational finance: This is going to include algorithmic trading, credit scoring, and fraud detection.
2. Computer vision and other parts of image processing. This can be used in some different parts like object detection, motion detection, and face recognition.
3. Computational biology. This is going to be used for a lot of different parts, including

DNA sequencing, drug discovery, and tumor detection.

4. Energy production. This can be used to help with a few different actions like load forecasting and to help predict what the prices will be.
5. Manufacturing, aerospace, and automotive options. This is going to be a great technique to work with when it comes to helping with many parts, including predictive maintenance.
6. Natural language processing: This is going to be the way that we can use machine learning to help with applications of voice recognition.

Machine learning and the algorithms that they control are going to work by finding some natural patterns in the data that you can use, including using it in a manner that will help us to make some better predictions and decisions along the way. They are going to be used on a daily basis by businesses and a lot of different companies in order to make lots of critical decisions.

For example, medical facilities can use this to help them to help diagnose patients. And we will find that there are a lot of media sites that will rely on machine learning in order to sift through the potential of millions of options in order to give recommendations to the users. Retailers can use this as a way to gain some insight into the purchasing behavior of their customers along the way.

There are many reasons that your business is able to consider using machine learning. For example, it is going to be useful if you are working with a task that is complex or one that is going to involve a larger amount of data and a ton of variables, but there isn't an equation or a formula that is out there right now to handle it. For example, some of the times when we want to work with machine learning include:

1. Equations and rules that are hand-written and too complex to work with. This could include some options like speech recognition and face recognition.
2. When you find that the rules that are going to change all of the time. This could be seen in actions lie fraud detection from a large number of transactional records.
3. When you find that the nature of your data is going to change on a constant basis, and the program has to be able to adapt along the way. This could be seen when we work with predicting the trends during shopping when doing energy demand forecasting and even automated trading, to name a few.

As you can see, there are a lot of different things that we are able to do when it comes to machine learning, and pretty much any industry is going to be able to benefit from working with this for their own needs. Machine learning is more complex, but we are able to combine it together with Python in order to get some amazing results in the process and to ensure that our data analysis is going to work the way that we want.

How Does Machine Learning Work with Data Analysis?

Now that we know a little bit more about how machine learning works and why it is important, it is time for us to take a look more specifically at how machine learning is able to come in and help us out with our data analysis. There are so many reasons why we are able to use machine learning when it comes to the data analysis, so it is important to take some time to look at how we can use it as well.

Machine learning is basically going to be the underlying process for all of the algorithms that we want to create along the way. No matter how simple or how complex your algorithm will be, a lot of the coding and the mechanics that come with it are going to really be run by the machine learning that we will talk about in this guidebook. And with the help of Python, you can make some really amazing algorithms that help us to sort through the data.

So, if you are actually hoping to go through this process of data analysis with the goal to sort through your data and understand what is found inside of it, then you need to learn a bit about machine learning ahead of time. The good news with this one is that machine learning is going to be able to work well with the Python language that we talked about above, ensuring that we can get it done with a simple coding language, even though the ideas that come with machine learning are going to be a bit more complex overall.

Supervised Machine Learning

The first type of learning that we need to take a look at here is known as supervised machine learning. This is going to be the most basic form of machine learning that we are able to work with, but it will provide us with some of the different parts that we need in order to keep things going well and can help us to train our algorithms in a quick and efficient manner.

To start, supervised learning is simply going to be the process of helping an algorithm to learn to map an input to a particular output. We are going to spend or time on this one while showing lots of examples, with the corresponding answers, to the algorithm in the hopes that it will find the connections and learn. Then, when the training is done, the algorithm will be able to look at new inputs, without the corresponding output, and give us the right answer on its own.

This whole process is going to be achieved when we work on a labeled data set that was collected earlier. If the mapping is done correctly, the algorithm is going to be able to learn in a successful manner. If it is not reaching the goals here, then that means we have to go through and make some changes to our algorithm to help it learn well. Supervised machine learning algorithms, when they are trained well, will be able to make some good predictions for the new data they get later on in the future.

This is going to be a similar process that we would see with a teacher to student scenario. There is going to be a teacher who is able to guide the student to learn well from books and other materials. The student is then going to be tested and, if they are correct, then the student will pass. If not, then the teacher will change things up and will help the student to learn better, so that they are able to learn from the mistakes that they made in the past so that they get better. This is going to be the basics that come with using supervised machine learning.

Unsupervised Machine Learning

The second type of machine learning that we are able to work with is known as unsupervised learning. This is going to be a method that we can use in data analysis because it will enable the machines to go through and classify both the tangible and intangible objects, without having to go through and provide the machine or the system with any information about of time about the objects.

The things or the objects that our machines are going to need to classify are going to be varied, such as the purchasing behaviors of the customer, some of the patterns of behavior of bacteria, and even things like hacker attacks or fraud happening with a bank. The main idea that we are going to be able to see with this kind of learning is that we want to expose our machines to large volumes of data that are varied and then allowing the algorithm to takes time to learn and infer from the data. However, we need to be able to take the time in order to teach the program how it can learn from that data.

It is pretty common for a computer system to need to learn how to make sense of large volumes of data, both the unstructured and the structured types, and then learn what insights are inside. In reality, it may be almost impossible to provide prior information about all of the data types that a system could receive over a period of time, and working with this kind of machine learning can help to make things happen, even when you are not able to train your machine ahead of time to teach it.

Keeping all of this in mind, we will find that supervised learning is not going to be all that suitable in every case, such as when the systems we are working with need to have a constant amount of information about data that is new. For example, hacking attacks on a bank or a financial system are going to frequently go through and change their patterns and their nature. Supervised learning would struggle with keeping up, but unsupervised learning is going to be more appropriate to handle this.

In these cases and more, unsupervised learning is going to be able to go onto a system and quickly learn from all of the data from the attack to keep up. Then it is able to infer and learn some more insights about potential future attacks, while also suggesting some preemptive actions to work with along the way.

There are a lot of times when we will want to work with unsupervised learning. Any time that you want to work with a program or a machine that needs to do at least a little bit of learning on its own in order to get things done, then unsupervised learning is going to be the right option to focus on.

Reinforcement Machine Learning

The third type of machine learning that we need to take a look at is known as reinforcement machine learning. This is going to be a bit different compared to what we saw with the other two options, but there are a lot of times when we can use this kind of learning to help us out with sorting through our data, including our data analysis. Let's dive into the basics of reinforcement machine learning and how we can use it for our needs.

To start, the reinforcement learning, in the context of artificial intelligence, is going to be a type of dynamic programming that is able to train algorithms, based on the idea of the reward when the algorithm gets the right answer, and a type of punishment when it gets the wrong answer.

One of the algorithms that use reinforcement learning, or the agent, is going to be able to learn how to interact with the environment that is going on around it. The agent or the algorithm is going to receive some kind of reward when it performs in the correct manner. But when it performs incorrectly, it is going to get some kind of punishment or penalty in the process. The agent, through these rewards and penalties, is going to learn, without any kind of intervention from a human, by maximizing its reward and then figuring out the best way to minimize the penalty that it is going to deal with.

The algorithm is going to be successful with this when it has a chance to learn the right way to behave, and the wrong way to behave. When it learns, through the rewards, the right way to behave, it will continue on with those actions or those guesses in order to get more rewards. And when it does get a penalty for doing something wrong, it is going to remember this as well and will learn how to avoid these along the way as well.

Reinforcement learning is going to be one of the approaches that we are able to use with machine learning, and the inspiration for it is going to be found in behaviorist psychology. We can view this in a manner that is similar to how a child is able to learn a new task. This learning is going to have some contrasts to how the other machine learning options will approach a situation because this particular algorithm is not going to be explicitly told how it should perform a task. It has to learn and go through this problem all on its own.

As an agent, which could be something like a program that is set up to play chess or a self-driving car, is going to interact with the environment that is all around it, and it is going to receive a type of reward state depending on how well it is able to perform. So, if the game is able to successfully win the game of chess, then it will receive a reward.

This goes the other way as well. if the agent does not perform in the manner that it should, whether that means that it doesn't win the game when it should, or does something else that is wrong based on the programming, then it is going to get a penalty of some sort. In the case of the game, it is going to be checkmated rather than winning, and it can learn from that in the process.

The agent, through more practice and over time, is going to be able to make some good decisions in order to maximize its rewards and minimize the number of times it gets a penalty through dynamic programming. The advantage of working with this kind of approach, especially when we work with artificial intelligence, is that it is going to allow our AI program to learn without the programming having to go through and spell out exactly how an agent should complete its own tasks.

As we can see, there are a lot of different parts that come together with the idea of machine learning, and being able to explore some of these and what we are able to do with the three main types of machine learning is going to be important based on how we want to use this in our own data analysis. Take some time to look more closely at how we can utilize all of the types of machine learning for our own needs, and move from there into using it to help pick out the algorithm we need to see success.

Chapter 10: Presenting the Results

This guidebook has taken some time to look at the different parts that come with data analysis. We looked at what the data analysis is all about and some of the benefits of working with this data analysis in the process. We took a look at what we can do with the Python coding language and explored some of the codings that we want to do with this language. And then, we went through some of the different steps that we need to explore in order to really see some results with our data analysis.

With all of that behind us, we now have some of the insights and the predictions that we need from all of this analysis. That still leaves us with another problem to deal with. We need to be able to take all of those insights and predictions and then figure out how to present it in a manner that those who are going to use that data, whether it is us, the shareholders, or others who are interested in the data, will be able to use and understand better.

When we get the data out from our algorithms, there is a wealth of information. But often, it is going to come out in a format that does not make a lot of sense if you are not a data scientist. Even if you are, there can be a lot of technical terms, and often we are going to end up with large reports with lots of technical parts that we need to know about.

We can go through and read this information, and there is not necessarily something that is wrong with this process along the way. But we do need to remember that this can be hard to read through, and will slow down some of the processes that we are working on here. We need to find some better methods to present the data, methods that will make it easier for us to look through the data, even at a glance, and understand what is there.

This is where the idea of data visuals is going to come in. There are a number of methods that we can use to help present the data that we want to work with, but nothing is going to be as effective as working with these data visuals. These will help us to sort through some of the insights and predictions that we have found along the way, and can make it so that we can see these connections at just a glance, rather than looking through and hoping that the reports and documents to find the same information.

To keep this simple, data visuals are going to just be a way to present our data in a graphical and pictorial format. It is going to help the decision-makers to see some of the analytics that are presented in a more visual manner, helping us to grasp some of the concepts that are more difficult, and can help us to identify some of the new patterns that are there.

We can even work with some of the visualizations that are out there. These are going to make it so that we can take our data visual process to another level by using a lot of different types of technology to drill down into the graphs and charts into as many details as possible. The interactivity that comes with these is going to make a big difference in the way that we are able to see data, and even in the manner that we process this data.

There are a lot of reasons that we need to be able to go through and use these data visuals. They are one of the best ways for us to go through and really understand the information that we processed through our algorithms as well. due to the method in which the brain is going to process information, working with graphs or charts to help us to visualize some of the larger amounts of complex data is going to be a lot easier than pouring over a lot of reports or spreadsheets in the process.

Compared to some of the other methods that are out there, you will find that these data visuals will be a quick and easy method to use when it is time to convey concepts in a manner that everyone is able to understand. It is even possible to take some of these visuals in order to experiment with some of the different scenarios possible, simply by going through and making some slight adjustments.

There are a number of things that these data visuals are going to be able to help us out with. Some of these will include:

1. They can help us to identify some of the areas that need more of our attention or some improvements.
2. They can make it easier to see which factors are the most likely to influence the behavior of a customer.
3. They will help us to understand where we should place all of our products.

4. They are great at going through and predicting some of the sales volumes that we need to work with along the way.

This brings us to the point of how we are able to use data visuals. No matter the type of industry that we are talking about, how the size of that industry, there are a lot of different types of businesses that are working with data visuals to make their data work better and to make more sense out of their data.

The first way that we are able to utilize these visuals is to make it possible to comprehend a lot of information in a quick manner. By using some of the graphs and charts to represent information for the business, these businesses find that it is easier to see large amounts of data in a clear and cohesive manner, and they will be able to draw some good conclusions from all of that information as well.

In addition, since it is going to be quite a bit faster to take information and analyze it when it turns into a graphical format, rather than having to go through and analyze it through the spreadsheets and documents that were traditionally used, businesses are able to address some of their major problems and answer questions in a more timely manner.

The next thing to work with is how data visuals are going to be able to help us go through and pinpoint some of the emerging trends. When we use these visuals in order to discover some of the trends, both in the market and in our own business, we will find that it is going to give us a good edge over our competition and that alone is going to be enough to help affect the bottom line. It is easier with these visuals to spot some of the outliers, especially the ones that are going to affect the customer churn or the quality of the customer, and then we can actually address them before they become really big issues.

We can also use these visuals to help identify some of the patterns and relationships that are found in our data. Even when we start to work with some of the large amounts of data that is complicated, we will find that they will make more sense when we present them in a graphical manner. With these visuals, it is even possible for a business to recognize the parameters that are there and are highly correlated.

Some of the different correlations that we will see with all of this will be pretty obvious to work with, but there are some that may be a bit more complicated to handle. Identifying these relationships are going to help a company to make plans to focus on the areas that are the most likely to influence the goals that are the most important to their goals.

And finally, we will find that the data visuals we are talking about here are going to be great options that help us to communicate our story in an efficient and fast manner to others. We can work with graphs, charts, and some of the other representatives of our data that are more graphical is going to be an important part of our data analysis because it is going to be really engaging and can help us to get the message out there a lot faster.

Before we get too far with our data visualization, we need to make sure that we are able to lay a bit of the groundwork as well. before we implement a bit of this new technology, there are going to be a number of steps that we have to go through and take. Not only do we want to make sure that we have a nice solid grasp on the data that we are working with and what we hope to see with it in the process, but we also need to have a good idea of our goals, needs, and audience as well.

Being able to prepare our company for this kind of technology is going to take some time and work as well. Some of the parts that have to come with this in order to make it work for our needs include:

1. We need to have a good understanding of the data that we need to visualize. This means that we need to know the size of the data we want to use. We also need to have a better idea of how unique the values in the data area or their cardinality.
2. Then we need to go through and determine the exact thing that we want to be able to visualize and have a good idea of the information type that we are hoping to communicate here.
3. Next, we need to make sure that we know as much about our audience as possible, and that we understand how that audience is going to be able to process all of that visual information.
4. Then we need to end this with a good knowledge of how we will use that visual in a manner that will help us to convey the information in the best form and the easiest form for others to handle as well.

Once we have been able to go through and answer these four questions about the data type that we would like to handle here, and the type of audience who will be looking at the data and the visuals, it is then time for us to go through and do a bit of preparation for the amount of data that we want to work with. Keep in mind that big data is often going to bring about a lot of new challenges to the visuals due to the different varieties that we want to use, the large volumes, and some of the varying velocities that we want to work with as well. Plus, it is also common for the data to get generated at a rate that is faster than we are able to manage it and analyze it, which is going to bring in another challenge to the mix.

There are also a few different factors that we want to handle here and consider to make the visual work. For example, we want to make sure to focus on the cardinality of the columns that we would like to visualize here. When we deal with high cardinality, that means that we will end up with a larger percentage of values in our set of data that are unique. This could be something like a data set of bank account numbers since we would expect each number to be different.

It is also possible for the data set we want to work with to be lower in the cardinality. This means that the column data that we are working with is going to come with a larger number or percentage of values that are able to repeat. This is something that is going to repeat on a frequent basis, such as the gender column in your data set.

While it may be a bit easier for us to go through and grasp some of the concepts that come with these data visuals and how it is going to help us out when it is time to take a lot of data and try to make sense of it. However, it is sometimes harder to understand what should come next and how you can create your own visuals. For example, what kinds of technology are you going to need and how you are able to use it for your needs.

There are a number of tools that we are able to use when it is time to create some of our own data visuals. The Matplotlib extension that works with the Python library is a great option to work with because it allows us to work on pretty much any of the different visuals that we want to handle, from charts and graphs and so much more. Pretty much any of the different options in visuals that you would like to focus on will be available with this library, and it allows you to use the simple Python language, which is going to make things so much easier for you.

Working with these data visuals is going to be important to our data analysis. It may not be the first thing that we think about when we handle some of the data analysis that we want to do here. And it is easy to think that it is not that important to start with. But it can make or break the project that you are handling when you get started.

These visuals are going to help us to go through and really understand what data is found in our algorithms, and instead of having to read through the documents and the spreadsheets that are out there with our insights and data, we can turn it into a visual and understand the complex relationships so much better. Whether we are using this for our own needs or presenting this to the owner of a business and their shareholders, you can't go wrong finishing up your data analysis with the help of some strong data visuals about that information.

Conclusion

Thank you for making it through to the end of *Python for Data Analysis*, I hope it was informative and able to provide you with all of the tools you need to achieve your goals whatever they may be.

The next step is to get started on working with your own data analysis. We spent a lot of time in this guidebook looking at what the data analysis is all about, some of the benefits of this analysis ad why a lot of different companies want to use this for their own needs, and even how to work through the steps of your own data analysis as well. Even as someone who is just getting started with data analysis and learning how to make this work for their own needs, you will find that this guidebook has all of the different tips and tricks and techniques that you need to see success.

In this guidebook, we took the time to look over a lot of the different things that we are able to do when it is time to work with data analysis. We looked at the benefits of the data analysis, some of the steps that we are able to use to get through this analysis and get the results that we want, and even how to work with things like the Python coding language and machine learning to get more out of our analysis as well. When all of this comes together, we are able to really show off our skills and enjoy all of the neat things that come with our analysis in the first place.

When you are ready to learn more about what a data analysis can do for you, and how you are able to work with this data analysis in order to get the best results, along with the Python language and machine learning, then it is time to take a look at what this guidebook has to offer!

Finally, if you found this book useful in any way, a review on Amazon is always appreciated!

www.ingramcontent.com/pod-product-compliance
Lightning Source LLC
Chambersburg PA
CBHW071407210526
45465CB00001B/283